| contemporary issues

# one way or many ways

**WHAT THE BIBLE SAYS ABOUT ETERNITY**

# paul chappell

Copyright © 2009 by Striving Together Publications. All Scripture quotations are taken from the King James Version.

First published in 2009 by Striving Together Publications, a ministry of Lancaster Baptist Church, Lancaster, CA 93535. Striving Together Publications is committed to providing tried, trusted, and proven books that will further equip local churches to carry out the Great Commission. Your comments and suggestions are valued.

All rights reserved. No part of this book may be reproduced, stored in a retrieval system, or transmitted in any form or by any means—electronic, mechanical, photocopy, recording, or otherwise—without written permission of the publisher, except for brief quotations in printed reviews.

Striving Together Publications
4020 E. Lancaster Blvd.
Lancaster, CA 93535
800.201.7748

Cover design by Andrew Jones
Layout by Craig Parker
Special thanks to our editorial team and proofreaders

ISBN 978-1-59894-089-3

Printed in the United States of America

# Contents

Introduction . . . . . . . . . . . . . . . . . . . . . . 5

1. The Nature of God . . . . . . . . . . . . . . . . . 11
2. The Promises of God . . . . . . . . . . . . . . . . 19
3. The Security of God . . . . . . . . . . . . . . . . 27

Conclusion . . . . . . . . . . . . . . . . . . . . . . 31

INTRODUCTION

As a pastor, I often have the opportunity to talk to people about weighty spiritual matters. Urging them to consider their spiritual condition, I often ask this question: "If you were to die today, would you go to Heaven or Hell, or do you know?" Many times the answer comes back, "Well, there are a lot of different ideas and opinions out there; how do you know you have the right answer?"

People are confused by the many different voices they are hearing, as the following excerpt from a television talk show reveals: "One of the mistakes that human beings make is believing that there is only one way to live, and that we don't accept that there are diverse ways of being in the world. There are… many paths to what you call God.…Her [a guest on the show] path might be something else.…But if her loving and her kindness and her generosity bring her to the same point that it brings you, it doesn't matter whether she called it God along the way or not.… there couldn't possibly be just one way."

Some of the most influential people in America believe that many different roads lead to Heaven, and statistics show that even those who sit in church pews are becoming confused by this philosophy. In a June 2008 *USA Today* article entitled, "Believers See Many Paths to Heaven," Cathy Grossman reported this new wave of religious thinking. She said, "Religion in the United States has a new anthem. No longer 'Give Me that Old Time Religion,' now it's 'Don't Fence Me in.' Newly released data from a major survey find that most American adults range far from knowing or caring about the distinctive teachings of their professed faith. They believe overwhelmingly (ninety-two percent) in God, and fifty-eight percent say they pray at least once a day. But when it comes to specific religions, they're all over the map."

Prominent people can preach their message over the airwaves, "All paths lead to Heaven!" But you must remember they are not the source of absolute truth. They are only people—people who make mistakes, just like you and me.

Maybe these voices have confused you too. Of all the paths of religion and supposed truth, which one leads to Heaven? Although you may feel you need to examine a plethora of internet information about every world religion, study piles of books, and visit countless churches, synagogues, and mosques to find the truth, the answer is simpler than you might imagine.

Because you were created with a God-shaped void in your heart, God is what your heart constantly yearns for. If you search your heart, you will realize He has already given you some understanding of Him. *"Because that which may be known of God is manifest in them; for God hath shewed it unto them."* (Romans 1:19). As you consider which path leads to Heaven, ask God to quiet all the other voices vying for your attention so that you can hear His voice alone.

How does God speak to human beings? He chose a people through whom He would reveal Himself to the world, He wrote a Book about His love for us, He etched Himself on our hearts, and most remarkable, He came to earth Himself.

If God has done so much to communicate His plan, then why is there so much confusion? God has an enemy. Satan rose up in rebellion against God and said, *"…I will ascend into heaven, I will exalt my throne above the stars of God: I will sit also upon the mount of the congregation, in the sides of the north: I will ascend above the heights of the clouds; I will be like the most High"* (Isaiah 14:13–14). Since then, he has actively plotted to introduce philosophies, concepts, and religions that compete with and diametrically oppose God and His truth. In other words, he offers many different roads to Heaven.

In the summer of 2006, our family had the opportunity to visit Europe. In Rome we saw the Pantheon—the Roman god house. This building is about two thousand years old. The ancient Romans brought their many different idols—Apollo, Zeus, and other deities of that era—to the Pantheon. Each worshipper could then choose a god to worship out of the broad selection represented in the Pantheon.

This philosophy, **polytheism,** is embraced by those who believe in and worship multiple deities. The word comes from the Greek *polytheoi,* which means "many gods."

When we compare historical accounts of polytheism to current cultural tendencies, we can see that western culture is succumbing to the same ideas. We attempt to put all religious systems on an equal level for the sake of unity. Unity that puts God on an equal plane with the Indian's sacred cow is unity at a very high cost—the souls of mankind.

Related to this philosophy is **pluralism**—the existence and availability of a number of world views, each vying for the allegiance of individuals, with no single world view dominant. A pluralist would say, "All religions are good; they are all about the same. Let's not emphasize any one set of beliefs." Pluralism sounds fair and egalitarian, but it is an insidious device. By *validating* all religions, it actually *discredits* them all, because all religions cannot be true—they disagree with one another! Of course, discrediting religion is exactly what Satan has in mind when he offers so many roads to Heaven.

Those who recognize that all religions cannot possibly be right often adopt a secular worldview. **Secularism,** according to *Mirriam-Webster's Collegiate Dictionary,* is the "indifference to or rejection or exclusion of religion and religious considerations." The secularist has no time for anything religious or biblical.

Others will pick and choose from each religion the components that suit them, creating their own belief system. But in so doing, they become their own gods. Whether or not they wear the label humanist, they are humanistic in their thinking. **Humanism** is the belief that man is his own god and his own conscience. It promotes the idea that man does not need the Bible or any other outside influence telling him what to do because he is essentially self-made. This philosophy is especially growing in our public educational system.

Satan has had his heyday. We can see the repercussions of these ploys more apparently with each generation—men and women drifting aimlessly with no real purpose in this life and no hope for the next.

Do you see any of these thought patterns in your own rationale? The answers to life's weightiest questions should not come from man-made belief systems such as polytheism, pluralism, secularism, or humanism. Society needs to return to this simple question: What does God say?

We are afforded a look into the heart of God as He reveals Himself to His chosen people, Israel. We can learn much from God's relationship to these people whom He chose to favor, because His relationship to them pictures another relationship—the one He wishes to have with you. God is looking for people to adopt into His family. He has already chosen you. The question is, will you choose Him?

## ONE

# THE NATURE OF GOD

Let me take you back 3,500 years to when the Israelites were enslaved in Egypt. The Israelites—the nation that God chose through which He would reveal Himself to the world—had been influenced by the idolatrous worship of the polytheistic culture in which they lived. God commissioned Moses to lead the Israelites out of Egypt on a three-day journey into the desert.

> *"And afterward Moses and Aaron went in, and told Pharaoh, Thus saith the* Lord *God of Israel, Let my people go, that they may hold a feast unto me in the wilderness. And Pharaoh said, Who is the* Lord, *that I should obey his voice to let Israel go? I know not the* Lord, *neither will I let*

*Israel go. And they said, The God of the Hebrews hath met with us: let us go, we pray thee, three days' journey into the desert, and sacrifice unto the LORD our God; lest he fall upon us with pestilence, or with the sword."*—EXODUS 5:1–3

The purpose of this journey was to remove the Israelites from the influence of the ancient Egyptians' religious practices so that God could reintroduce Himself to His people. God wanted His children to worship Him as the one true God.

After miraculously bringing the Israelites out of Egypt, God explained that the basis of His blessing upon their nation would be that they worship Him and Him alone. The first commandment He gave to His people reveals His heart: *"Thou shalt have no other gods before me. Thou shalt not make unto thee any graven image, or any likeness of any thing that is in heaven above, or that is in the earth beneath, or that is in the water under the earth"* (Exodus 20:3–4).

He chose to love Israel, and He desired their love in return. *"Hear, O Israel: The LORD our God is one LORD: And thou shalt love the LORD thy God with all thine heart, and with all thy soul, and with all thy might"* (Deuteronomy 6:4–5). In telling the Israelites His name, God explains why He alone is worthy of their devotion.

## God's Name

In Bible days, children were given names that had significant meanings. Sometimes after a critical life event, people changed their names to reflect the change in them. People associated the meaning of a name with the person.

When God commissioned Moses to lead the Israelites out of Egypt, He gave Moses His name. *"And God said unto Moses, I AM THAT I AM: and he said, Thus shalt thou say unto the children of Israel, I AM hath sent me unto you"* (Exodus 3:14).

The name "I AM" speaks of God's self-sufficiency. He has no beginning or end. Isaiah 63:16 says, *"…thy name is from everlasting."* "I AM" revealed that God has the attributes of deity, the power over His creation.

> *"O LORD our Lord, how excellent is thy name in all the earth! who hast set thy glory above the heavens.…When I consider thy heavens, the work of thy fingers, the moon and the stars, which thou hast ordained; What is man, that thou art mindful of him? and the son of man, that thou visitest him?"*—PSALMS 8:1, 3–4

He is a self-existent, self-sufficient God. *"His name shall endure for ever…"* (Psalms 72:17).

God alone is worthy to receive worship. He is high and lifted up. No one else can claim to be the "I AM," the Creator, God. Except One. *"Jesus said unto them, Verily, verily, I say unto you, Before Abraham was, I am"* (John 8:58). Who is Jesus Christ? Is He God?

The Bible is very clear on the identity of Jesus. In the Old Testament, God referred to Himself as "I AM," and in the New Testament, Jesus Christ said, "*…Before Abraham was, I am.*" Jesus again stated in John 10:30, *"I and my Father are one."*

John 1:14 explains more fully, *"And the Word was made flesh, and dwelt among us, (and we beheld his glory, the glory as of the only begotten of the Father,) full of grace and truth."* *Word* in this verse is speaking of the eternal Word—Jesus Christ. Note how the Word, referring to Jesus, is used in succession in the following verses:

> *"In the beginning was the Word, and the Word was with God, and the Word was God. The same was in the beginning with God. All things were made by him; and without him was not any thing made that was made."*—John 1:1–3

Jesus existed in the beginning. He was with God. He *is* God—the Creator of the universe. Deity wrapped Himself in humanity and came to this earth to live among us.

Many people want to have God in their lives, but they want to have Him in their own way. They want to travel their own paths—paths that contradict God's truth about Heaven and deny that Jesus Christ is God. But God is who He is, not who we want Him to be. We must learn from the Bible who God is and then follow the one path He has chosen.

What is that path? God Himself came to make a way for us to go to Heaven. Jesus is the way—the one path that leads to Heaven. *"Jesus saith unto him, I am the way, the truth, and the life: no man cometh unto the Father, but by me"* (John 14:6).

God chose to lift up the name of Christ because He is God—God robed in flesh.

> *"Wherefore God also hath highly exalted him, and given him a name which is above every name: That at the name of Jesus every knee should bow, of things in heaven, and things in earth, and things under the earth; And that every tongue should confess that Jesus Christ is Lord, to the glory of God the Father."*—Philippians 2:9–11

God's name plays an important role regarding the subject of which way is the right way. His name reveals to us His attributes, His being, and His oneness with Jesus Christ.

## God's Nature

The account of the conversation God had with Moses is found in Exodus 3:2, *"And the angel of the Lord appeared unto him in a flame of fire out of the midst of a bush: and he looked, and, behold, the bush burned with fire, and the bush was not consumed."*

As Moses saw the bush on fire, but not consumed, he saw a picture of God's nature. He is forever the same, forever unchanging. Men's philosophies come and go, but our self-existent God remains unchanged.

God is also all-powerful. Jesus explained this truth in Matthew 28:18, *"And Jesus came and spake unto them, saying, All power is given unto me in heaven and in earth."* God gave Jesus power over sickness and unclean spirits, even over death (Acts 10:38). The most amazing power He has is the power to forgive (Luke 5:24). He can take a life diseased with sin and make it whole again.

I will never forget one of my first marriage counseling experiences. As a new assistant pastor, just starting out in ministry, I answered the church phone the day a gentleman called asking for an appointment. We scheduled a counseling session for him and his wife, and not long after our phone conversation, I was sitting in the office with this couple.

I felt as prepared as I could be. I had reviewed my college notes on marriage counseling, and I selected the best verses on marriage. One of the first questions I asked this couple was how long their marital problems had lasted.

"Ten years," they replied.

Next, I asked how long they had been married. Their answer was the same, "Ten years."

With some hesitation, I asked, "Exactly when did your marital problems begin?"

The wife answered, "The day we got married."

When I inquired about the history of their relationship, I learned they had grown up in India. The wife's father had gone to the market and met the husband's father. They swapped currency, shook hands, and arranged the marriage of their children. The young people complied, but they had no foundation for their relationship except obedience to their parents.

At that point, I did not analyze their current marital problems one-by-one because these problems were only superficial. They had a problem that went much deeper—their sin. I showed them from the Bible how to lay a solid foundation for their marriage—a foundation built upon Jesus Christ.

Coming from the polytheistic background of India, this dear couple had to start from the very beginning to learn about Jesus Christ and God. Initially, they wanted to accept Jesus like they would accept an elephant or a locust. He would have been an addition to their many gods. For a few weeks we studied together what the Bible says about Jesus Christ and His eternal existence.

As this couple grew in the knowledge of Jesus Christ, they soon realized the only hope for their marriage was first to deal with their root problem. They both bowed their heads and accepted the payment Christ made for their sin. Only when they turned their backs on all their other gods, were they able to trust the all-powerful God of the Bible— the God who was able to make a real difference in their lives.

I encourage you to place your eternal destination in the hands of the God of the Bible, for His deity far surpasses any gods or philosophies configured by man.

## TWO

# THE PROMISES OF GOD

Corrie ten Boom, a survivor of a Nazi concentration camp, once said, "Let God's promises shine on your problems." This is good advice to those unsure of their eternal destination. For within the Bible, God promises we can know that we have eternal life.

Let's travel back again to the time in Egypt when God told the children of Israel to leave on a three-day journey. It was at this time that God promised to deliver His people out of the slavery they endured in Egypt. This historic account of the Israelites' deliverance from Egypt pictures the deliverance God has promised to give us.

## God Promised to Deliver His People

During our trip to Europe, my family and I visited a British museum where we saw a brick stamped "King Ramses II" on top. Recognizing that this brick was from the very era when the Egyptians forced the Israelites into heavy labor, I was touched to realize that the blood and sweat of Israelite slaves had produced this relic we were now viewing.

God heard the cries of these oppressed and persecuted people.

> *"And the* Lord *said, I have surely seen the affliction of my people which are in Egypt, and have heard their cry by reason of their taskmasters; for I know their sorrows; And I am come down to deliver them out of the hand of the Egyptians, and to bring them up out of that land unto a good land and a large, unto a land flowing with milk and honey; unto the place of the Canaanites, and the Hittites, and the Amorites, and the Perizzites, and the Hivites, and the Jebusites."*—Exodus 3:7–8

You might say, "How does this ancient story about Israelite slaves relate to me? I'm not in bondage."

The Bible tells us about bondage to the world's religious systems: *"Even so we, when we were children, were in bondage under the elements of the world"* (Galatians 4:3). The word *elements* is referring to the demands of the world's religious philosophies. Religion constantly burdens its followers with requirements for entrance into Heaven. Some religions teach that you must be baptized to reach Heaven. Others teach that you must confess your sins to a priest or give a certain amount yearly to the church. Some teach that your good must outweigh your bad.

In a nutshell, religion teaches that if you do enough good works, you may get to go to Heaven. How much is enough? Which religion has the right requirements? Can anyone really buy Heaven?

God hears you crying out for answers. Just as God delivered His people from the bondage of Egypt, He wants to deliver you from the questions that flood your mind and keep you up at night. He wants to be your answer, and He wants to be your God. He promises to deliver you from your greatest burden—the burden of sin.

## God Promises to Deliver Us from Sin

The greatest burden of every man, woman, boy, and girl is the burden of sin. Someone once said, "If our greatest need had been information, God would have sent us an educator. If our greatest need had been technology, God would have sent us a scientist.

If our greatest need had been political, God would have sent us a politician. But our greatest need was forgiveness, so God sent us a Saviour."

Romans 3:23 says, *"For all have sinned, and come short of the glory of God."* Because we are all sinners, we fall short of God's standard of righteousness—perfection. I can work really hard to be a good person, but I am going to fall short. I can get baptized, but when I come out of the water, I am going to be a wet sinner. I can give every penny I have to the church, but when I leave, I'm going to be a destitute sinner. I can crawl up hundreds of stairs on my hands and knees to do penance, but when I get up, I'm going to be a maimed sinner. The fact is, no matter what I do, I am a sinner, and sinners can't go to Heaven.

God, because He is just and holy, had to put a penalty on sin. *"For the wages of sin is death…"* (Romans 6:23). When sin entered the world, so did death—physical death and spiritual death. *"And death and hell were cast into the lake of fire. This is the second death. And whosoever was not found written in the book of life was cast into the lake of fire."* (Revelation 20:14–15).

Some people say, "Well, I just don't think I'm that bad." How many sins does it take to be a sinner? Just one. We all fall short. First John 1:8 says, *"If we say that we have no sin, we deceive ourselves, and the truth is not in us."*

God looked through eyes of compassion and saw us in our pathetic condition—lost in sin and unable to help ourselves. His holiness said, "Sin must be paid for." His love said, "I'll pay for it Myself." The Prince of Heaven cloaked His glory in humble flesh. He left the splendor of Heaven to live amidst the degradation of mankind. He was mocked, ridiculed, betrayed, tortured, mutilated, and nailed to a cross to die a horrific death. Why? *"But God commendeth [proved] his love toward us, in that, while we were yet sinners, Christ died for us"* (Romans 5:8).

God loved you so much He sent his only begotten Son to die on the Cross to pay the penalty for your sin. There was no other way—no other path to Heaven. Sin had to be paid for, and Jesus Christ was the only One qualified to pay for your sins because He was the only sinless person ever to walk this planet. He didn't owe a penalty for His own sin as you and I do—He had no sin.

Now God is offering you a gift. He is offering to cover your sin—to robe you in the righteousness of Christ so that He cannot see your sin any longer. He is offering eternal life in Heaven as a gift—no strings attached: *"…the gift of God is eternal life through Jesus Christ our Lord"* (Romans 6:23). Religion requires payment for salvation, but Christ offers it as a gift.

Ephesians 2:8-9 says, *"For by grace are ye saved through faith; and that not of yourselves: it is the gift of*

*God: Not of works, lest any man should boast."* I am so glad that I don't have to earn my way to Heaven.

You still have a choice to make. When you are offered a gift, you have one of two options—you can reject it or accept it. You can say, "I'll pay for my own sins in hell." Or you can say "I accept the payment that Jesus made on my behalf."

You might reason, "That's too easy. There has to be more." What more could you ask for? Could God have done more than sacrifice His own Son? It wasn't easy; it was a very high price to pay. God's part is grace—He forgives us though we do not deserve it. Our part is faith—we put our faith in the Lord Jesus Christ to be saved.

God is not the author of confusion. He made salvation available to all men—one way, a simple way.

> *"And this is the record, that God hath given to us eternal life, and this life is in his Son. He that hath the Son hath life; and he that hath not the Son of God hath not life. These things have I written unto you that believe on the name of the Son of God; that ye may know that ye have eternal life, and that ye may believe on the name of the Son of God."*—1 JOHN 5:11–13

The path to Heaven is God's Son. Eternal life hinges on what you do with the claims of Jesus Christ. If you follow cultural trends, believing that there are many roads to Heaven, you are rejecting Jesus Christ. Please understand that Christ is not one of many options. He is your only option. He is *"the way, the truth, and the life"* (John 14:6).

How can you be assured that Heaven will one day be your home? God promises to redeem you from your sin, but you must respond to this promise.

THREE

# THE SECURITY OF GOD

You can trust God. If you want your sins forgiven and Heaven to be your eternal destination, trust in Christ. The Bible speaks of Jesus in Acts 4:12: *"Neither is there salvation in any other: for there is none other name under heaven given among men, whereby we must be saved."*

Some people have trouble putting their whole faith in Jesus Christ. There is something about our human nature that says, "I realize that I need to believe in Jesus Christ, but just in case I'm wrong, there must be something else I can do." These people surmise that to get to heaven they can add something to their faith in Jesus. They trust Jesus and get baptized and do good works and keep the Ten Commandments and give money to charities and…the list could go on. If you add anything else to simple faith in Christ, you are not trusting in Christ but in your works. Romans 11:6 explains the exclusivity of grace and works, *"And if by grace, then is it no more of works: otherwise grace is no more grace. But if it be of works, then is it no more grace: otherwise work is no more work."* You are either trusting in your works or in the grace of God—one or the other.

If there were anything man could do to save himself, Jesus' cruel death would have been unnecessary, but there is nothing but the blood of Christ that can pay for our sins.

Many paths claim Heaven as their final destination, but only one path leads to Heaven. The Bible says in 1 Timothy 2:5, *"For there is one God, and one mediator between God and men, the man Christ Jesus."*

Are you ready to put your faith in God and God alone? If you are ready to take this step, then follow the instruction Romans 10:9–10 gives, *"That if thou shalt confess with thy mouth the Lord Jesus, and shalt believe in thine heart that God hath raised him from the dead, thou shalt be saved. For with the heart man believeth unto righteousness; and with the mouth confession is made unto salvation."*

Romans 10:13 says, *"For whosoever shall call upon the name of the Lord shall be saved."* Simply admit to God that you are a sinner and that you believe Jesus is the Son of God who died on the cross to pay for your sin; then call on Him and ask Him to save you. Pray something like this:

> *Dear God, I know that I am separated from You because of sin. I confess that in my sin I cannot save myself. Right now, I turn to You alone to be my Saviour. I ask You to save me from the penalty of my sin, trusting the payment You made when You died on the Cross for me.—Amen*

If you just asked Jesus Christ to be your Saviour, you have entered a relationship that is as secure as the promises of God. Your sins are forgiven, never again to be held against you. Take a few moments to read John chapter 10 and learn how Christ takes care of those to whom He gives eternal life.

CONCLUSION

The first time I met someone who had the "many roads lead to Heaven" philosophy, I was a teenager.

Our youth group was very evangelistic, often going into the community to tell others about Jesus Christ. One rainy day, my youth pastor directed our youth group onto a bus and announced that we were going to the Eastridge Mall in San Jose, California. The mall provided a dry place where we could pass out brochures that explained the truth about eternity.

When we reached the mall, the teens began to file off the bus. As I stepped out, I spotted a lady nearby in the parking lot. I walked up to her, handed her a brochure, and invited her to one of our services. Then I said, "Ma'am, do you mind if I ask you a question?"

"Go right ahead," she said.

"Ma'am, do you know that if you were to die, whether you would spend eternity in Heaven, in Hell, or do you know?"

"Son," she began, "let me explain it to you this way. Heaven is a lot like this mall. There are a lot of roads that lead to this mall, and any one of them will get you to the mall. There are a lot of different religions, but ultimately, they will all lead you to Heaven."

If her philosophy is true, there is no need to read the Bible, attend church, or seek the correct path to Heaven. But her philosophy is not true. It stems from man's derived opinions and ideas, not from absolute truth.

As we conclude this study, I challenge you to make the popular question "Which path leads to Heaven?" a matter of personal faith. Choose the one true God—Jesus Christ—the One who created you, loved you, and died for you. *"For God so loved the world, that he gave his only begotten Son, that whosoever believeth in him should not perish, but have everlasting life"* (John 3:16).

Have you trusted Christ as your personal Saviour as a result of this book? If so, we would like to send you a gift copy of the Bible as well as a copy of the workbook *First Steps for New Christians*.

Please contact us as soon as possible so we can rejoice in your decision and send you these tools for growth in your new relationship with God.

| | |
|---|---|
| **Write:** | Striving Together Publications<br>4020 E. Lancaster Blvd.<br>Lancaster, CA 93535 |
| **Call:** | 800.201.7748 |
| **Email:** | strive@lancasterbaptist.org |
| **Go online:** | www.strivingtogether.com |

# Wayside Temple
3809 Maple Ave
Castalia, Ohio 44824
419.684.5311

### Service Times:
Sunday School | 9:30am
Morning Worship | 10:30am
Sunday Evening | 6:00pm
Wednesday Night | 7:00pm

If our church family can be of service to you, or if you need answers to spiritual questions, please do not hesitate to contact our office as soon as possible. May the Lord bless you.

*Pastor Rusty Yost*

For more info visit.

# cbmtoday.org

# ABOUT THE AUTHOR

 Paul Chappell is the senior pastor of the Lancaster Baptist Church and president of West Coast Baptist College in Lancaster, California. His biblical vision has led the church to become one of the most dynamic independent Baptist churches in the nation, and his Christ-centered leadership philosophy has become a model for hundreds of future leaders currently training at West Coast Baptist College.

# Additional Contemporary Issues booklets available from
# Striving Together Publications

### The Biblical Sanctity of Life

When does life begin? Nobody wants to answer this question. Our courts cannot decide. Our government cannot decide. Our educational institutions cannot decide. Even our pulpits are growing more and more silent on the value of life in the womb. But God answered this question a long time ago. Have you ever heard His thoughts on the matter? This booklet opens the pages of the Bible and allows God to clearly and powerfully answer the question—when does life begin? (40 pages, booklet)

### Exposing the Deception of Humanism

Humanism is the belief that man is his own god, and outside of mankind, we need no higher deity or authority. Proponents of humanism are active in government and education, attempting to remove God from society. This booklet exposes the emptiness behind the message that mankind is his own savior, and it charts a path away from the error and back to the truth of Jesus Christ. Learn the core beliefs of this growing religious movement, and discover how to reject its deception. (48 pages, booklet)

### The Blessings and Pitfalls of Social Networking

In this booklet, we examine two angles of social networking—some of the potential blessings and many of the potential pitfalls. We conclude our study by applying several timeless scriptural principles to this emerging technology. (48 pages, booklet)

# Additional Contemporary Issues booklets available from
# Striving Together Publications

### Does God Care What We Wear?

God accepts us just as we are—His love is unconditional and independent of our behavior or appearance. But does this mean that He doesn't care about our clothing choices? Our culture is continually dressing down—"sleazier and sloppier" seems to be the motto of the day, even for Christians. But is this really pleasing to God? Does it even matter to Him? After all, He sees the heart, right? The pages of this booklet will challenge your thinking with eleven biblical principles and well-applied truths. Together we will explore what the Bible really says about what we wear. (32 pages, booklet)

### Biblical Guidelines for Using the Internet

The internet has changed our twenty-first century world! It has changed relationships, homes, businesses, and individuals. The challenges of using the internet appropriately are growing every day, as is the cultural and generational divide between parents and children in how they understand and use the internet. This booklet will provide you with a biblical perspective and practical steps for using the internet safely and appropriately as a Christian. (48 pages, paperback)

## For more books, minibooks, curriculum, and resources for Christian growth, visit

## strivingtogether.com

# Visit us online

strivingtogether.com

dailyintheword.org

wcbc.edu

lancasterbaptist.org

paulchappell.com